MW01077833

Nach mittlerweile 13 Jahren Graffiti, fast die Hältfe meines Lebens, bin ich jeden Tag aufs neue begeistert und beeindruckt, was diese urbane Kunst für Formen und Strukturen gebildet hat und wieviel Ausdruck und Kraft dahinter steckt.
Das entschädigt all die Tiefschläge, die man ertragen, und Dinge auf die verzichtet werden muss.
Dieses Buch ist all meinen Freunden gewidmet, die ich versetzt habe, meinen Eltern, die mich nicht verstehen können, den Frauen, die ich enttäuscht habe, und den Parties, auf denen ich nicht war.

[MC]

>Ich habe nichts zu sagen, deshalb male ich< sba.hamburg
I got nothing to say, that's why I'm writing

STYLEFILE.BLACKBOOK.SESSIONS
Graffiti on paper
Publikat KG
Aschaffenburg, 08.2002
2. Auflage: 12.2002
Redaktion & Layout: Markus Christl

Publikat Verlags- und Handels KG
Erthalstrasse 11
D-63739 Aschaffenburg
Germany
www.stylefile.de
mailorder@stylefile.de

Vorliegendes Werk nimmt sich nicht dem gesprühten Bild auf der Wand oder Zug, sondern der Vorstufe dazu, den Sketchen auf Papier, an.

Durch das ständig wachsende Phänomen Graffiti bietet auch diese Sparte dem Betrachter eine unglaubliche Bandbreite. Während für manche die Skizze lediglich ein "Sprühplan" ist, zelebrieren andere die Zeichnung wiederum als echte Alternative zur Arbeit mit der Dose. Dies verdeutlichen die vielen, liebevoll ausgearbeiteten Sketches, die nachfolgend präsentiert werden.

Aber um auch die Essenz der Skizzen, das Entwickeln und vor allem Weiterentwickeln der eigenen Handschrift zu verdeutlichen, war es uns wichtig auch Scribbles abzubilden. Schnelle Gedanken, schemenhaft skizziert, verworfen, neu angesetzt... "Try and error" als Weg, den eigenen Style voranzubringen. Skizzen mit all ihren Stärken und Schwächen. Diese ganz persönlichen Einblicke waren bisher nur dem engen Bekanntenkreis der Writer als Diskussionsgrundlage vorbehalten, sind jedoch das Fundament eines jeden ausgefeilten Styles.

Mit BLACKBOOK.SESSIONS öffnen wir nun sowohl die Bücher der international renomierten Writergemeinde als auch die der neuen Generationen.

Viel Spaß beim Studieren und Genießen dieser Arbeiten.

Graffiti is a huge growing phenomenon itself, whether in the area of steel, walls or sketches. The sketches presented here do not represent the painted piece on the wall or train, but rather the preliminary stage before it. While some sketches are only plans, others are "celebrations" and alternatives to painting on a wall. Some artists do not even paint and choose to draw in blackbooks alone. This shows that some sketches can be works of art themselves, because they can be just as complex as a piece on a wall and train.

For us it is important to show the evolving and the ongoing process with writing from sketches to the finished pieces. These include quick thoughts, sketched in scenes, and other ideas that have come with trail and error to get to the final style you see, evolved. The sketches you see here are sketches in the rough, with all their strengths and weaknesses. While these were once reserved for a small personal circle of friends a foundation to study and build their skills from, and something to discuss, this once private raw style is now yours to study.

In BLACKBOOK.SESSIONS we open the books of international famous writer and also the ones from the new generation.

We hope you enjoy.

[stylefile-blackbook-squad]

[bus126.berlin]

JACK ODEM MILK...

BUS126

[diak.berlin]

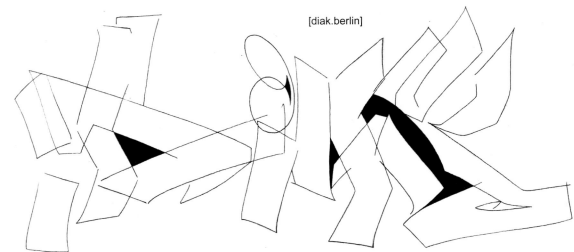

[jack.berlin]

[recycle.berlin]

[zound.berlin]

[irak.berlin]

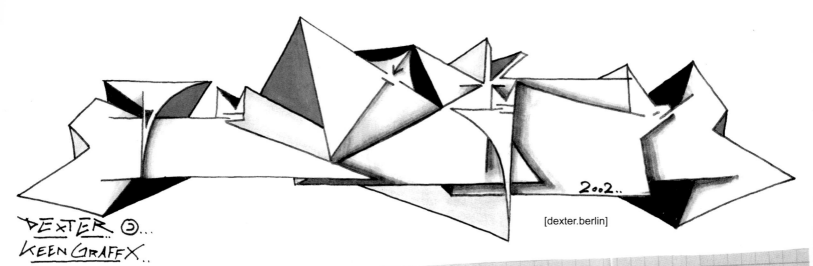

DEXTER ③...
KEEN GRAFFX...

[dexter.berlin]

KHC   DSF

Relax 2002

[relax.berlin]

[skim.berlin]

[eco.berlin]

[porno.berlin]

9 times out of 10 i win...

BigFAB

Reminis...

Mystik Journeymen

Eligh

Hobo Junction

"Never Loose Touch"...

The Grouch

[sure.berlin]

VON ZITZE.WITZ BIN DEUTSCHER.

[kent.frankfurt]

[paw.aachen]

2oo2 ©

[toxin.karlsruhe]

[slave.stuttgart]

[cesm.frankfurt]

[power.hamburg]

Wikked-Kreations.com

[tns_by_htl.munich]

[filou.berlin]

[ritual.berlin]

[fiend.nuernberg]

[alois.nuernberg]

[nomad.nuernberg]

[django.nuernberg]

[fiend.nuernberg]

Motherfuckers know who's the best!
If it's ain't the KSD, it must be the MOAS!

can't believe that I'm here… here we are, win or lose, good and bad, fast and loose… (motörhead).

…So here I am at last I can tell what I want - what I always wanted to say, but what?

About style… everything is relative and a matter of taste, for me the only thing that matters is harmony, (aero)dynamic and swing. About sketching and so on… let´s go....

In the beginning I always said I´m untalented and I'm only in it for some fun, bombing and everything; I don´t have to practise for this short flash. What I didn´t know was that I was already infected by this virus. At first I noticed with bombing that I had to practise, while I never envolved that much style that it was satisfying. I´ve also belonged to the ones who said: "Hall of fame… That´s for pussies. Bombing is the real thing." The same thing you still hear every day. I realized quickly that the big Jimboleddy had lots of fun and energy for style, but no skills. That was kind of embarrasing.

A different problem was that Berlin was not close by, and there was no local train system unlike in other cities… damn, I was marked by Berlin - RASTA once did a burner on the station with crazy flow (but don´t tell anyone). Blablabla… now it´s getting important. There was an oldschooler, his name was "Idiot Ol Oldenburg" . He taught me two things: First the more antisocial the better it is and second do five sketches a day and you´ll get good, no matter what, practice to write your name… he was right, but there were also some negative aspects or funny… I paint/ draw my ass off even after work and with probation, and what do I get? Friends from all over the bananarepublic ask me if I had a bad day on this panel in the last Backspin; and I would always paint a name with sense. SEMAK , what's that… airplane, bird… no it´s JIMBO and someone did not practise enough!!! (like many others)…

Through all the sketching, I noticed that I did stylemoves like the ones of KENT, WOW or AIDS - but those were mine. I never insisted on it. As a toy you don´t do something like that, you have to show respect to age and experience. I thought: "Ok, this is how he got to this one". I knew I was on the right way and my time would come. It gave me some fine energy-flashes and made it easier to show some patience. Something that gets lost very often in this time. I have used experiences to find my own thing. I learned how to get to styles, wild-styles made of letters like the ones written down here.

In some magazines I am only talented in blackbooks - but it´s also that way with drin-king beer!! (DIKO, SONS, J-CAP and JET tought me how to do it - thanks, the time with you was great).

No guys, stay serious. It´s true, I´m the cra-ziest in blackbooks (#26 in fullcolor is coming). But I tell you one thing: It is f***ing hard and sometimes I put spells on the sketch which was better than the one before and I forced myself never to do a worse one. Battle forever with myself on my way to eternity.

´m also known for some crazy blackbookstuff and some ill shit. I do this only to define my-self as a serious artist. No, this only helps me a lot with planning colors and proportions for the style on the wall. I just expect to see on the wall that there is something wrong… and sometimes I get an idea even though of my age and my job in psychiatry… I rather test

those in the book than having to laugh about myself. But still things come up spontaneous-ly. But on with the text… I met some great wri-ters, who are also personally first choice… in the area of style besides BTN- and SIM-crew of Bremerhaven and WB-crew of Bremen. First DIKO of the Mühlenberg-tram-corner, who was with me for the first time out for tag-, throw up-, onlinestyle-, stylebattle and so on and who really kicked my ass. Memories that had shown me back then that I had no idea at all about style! And second DISKO of the Schmuckstreet in Hamburg, from the occult bloodsect, who (and I´m sorry for all the maga-zinepopstars) puts everyone in second place when it´s about allroundskills (thanks for the tattoo - DerSUperDicKeFlash"). Do you know what is the bad thing? I believe these guys are not intrested in all this bullshit - go on like this. Modesty rules and friendship is better than 10.000 trains.

In the end something bad: You can all come with 10.000 trains and/or worked out (but soul-less) conceptwalls, but TOBAK of Hamburg burns you all with one throw-up. He worked on himself till he puked and still he stayed down low! And the result of all this crap: Try, try, try, to put your styles in shapes and sometimes begin from right or or or… and two more things why sketching makes sense: First everyone will tell you that it is nice and neat, but no one is as good in the book as JYM and second, I´m someone who puts himself up and lets ATOM do the rest (Don´t ever do that again), ok, batt-le. I always wanted to be able to write every letter. Therefore I had to use the book, becau-se I had to paint as much as "he"… and HITME said: JIMMY, you made the dirty style

known in the BRD …", but no!! it was AHOI or CHR-crew from the fucked up major city in Niedersachen (I hope you are alright - wishes for your marriage). Peace, piece and cheers…LEDDY

"JYM 129"

P.S.: these lines are dedicated for DJ MIRKO MACHINE (Fuck Spax, you get shit in your mail), because he a) scratches heavy metal samples and b) because he put on the funny splashfest Spax´ groupies (his?) on the "white god"… you can all come back with a black-book, I don´t do autographes, I do tags! But MIRKO is not a good example in the context of sketching. He has been trying for years, but is not getting better, that´s why my characters always cry.

P.P.S.: The characters really cry, because peo-ple like SONS, AHOI, NEST, KARE, MONEY, TRIAL, MSYM, ENTER, RISK, SUCK, CASH, REIM, FORDY, DIKO, DEAK, DISKO, PHORE, RISE and so on don´t get the right attention - you are better than the rest and even better than me……

Greetings to JOEY and ELVIS (still waiting for Lemmy) and then rock´n´roll.

HAPZ, COScrew, BTN´s, 13ers, WB´s, SIM´s, OCB´s, AMB´s, DSUDKF, KingEAS, my crews… Monsters of art, (VIMS, MSN, ALL, TKO), Born to Porn, StylisTIX (Mias, Este,Diko), RSK (yo Soer), Metal Fuckers (MONK, ATOM, KARE, JEKS) and of course my heart, KSDcrew (EISER get going), and SPECIAL and my brothers DJ MIRKO and MC SENZKE… ACE, REAL, GOBLIN… BJOHAN, SEAK, JOSH (you can´t separate us) and last but not least CAPTAIN STARRIN

[recycle.berlin]

[tumor.munich]

trashmark merchandising GmbH.fon: +49(0)231 9371110 fax: +49(0)231 9371112 email:info@trashmark.com

[joan&krixl.aschaffenburg]

[fister.erfurt]

[porno.berlin]

[super.munich]

[kiam.karlsruhe]

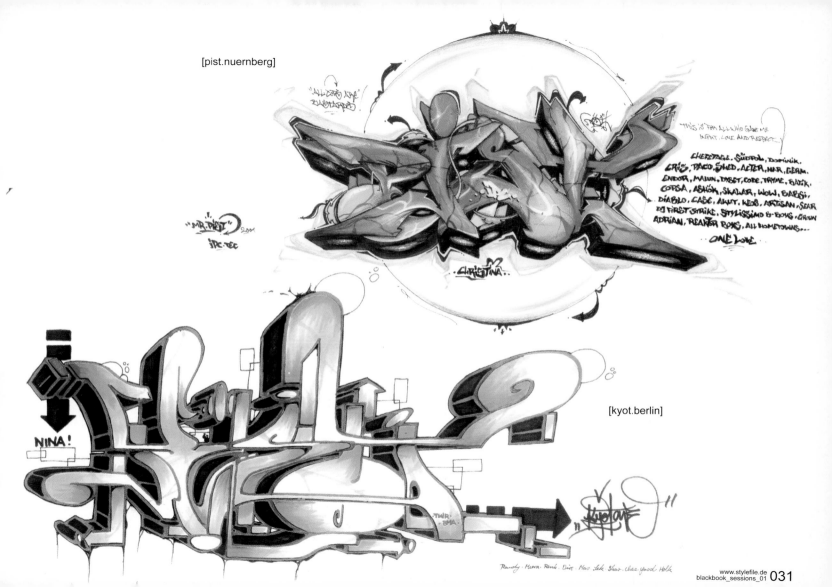

[pist.nuernberg]

[kyot.berlin]

NINA!

[power.hamburg]

[<rise.hamburg]

[fred.gifhorn]

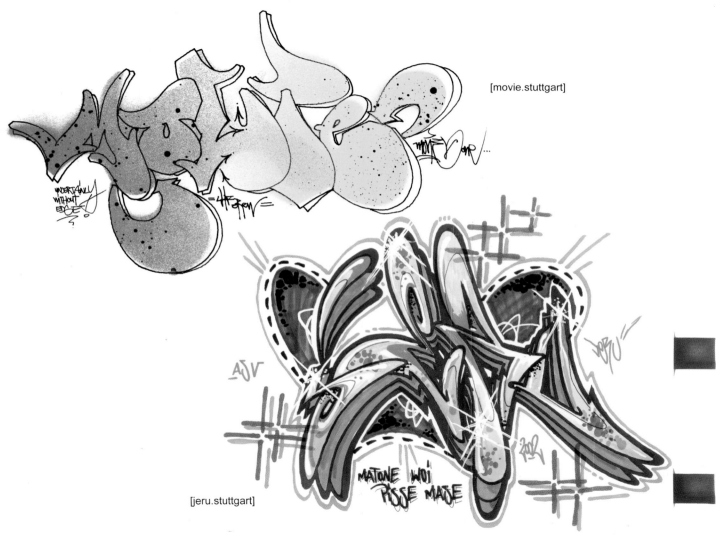

[movie.stuttgart]

[jeru.stuttgart]

[paw.aachen]

[town.nuernberg]

[bone.berlin]

[2fast.berlin]

[stuka.braunschweig]

[dream.basel]

...FOR DARE / the WILD SIDE

..SZR.KIM.123K..

Silvia...

DARE.KESY.SPLASH.ECB.

Schen&Klor.CESM..
KETSAR

..2002..

[reso.saarbruecken]

[dare.basel]

ANYTIME...ANYWHERE
...DARE...

"181201 →THE WILD SIDE"

WWW.COPIC.DE

COPIC
MARKER · CIAO · VARIOUS INK

[hejduk.sweden]

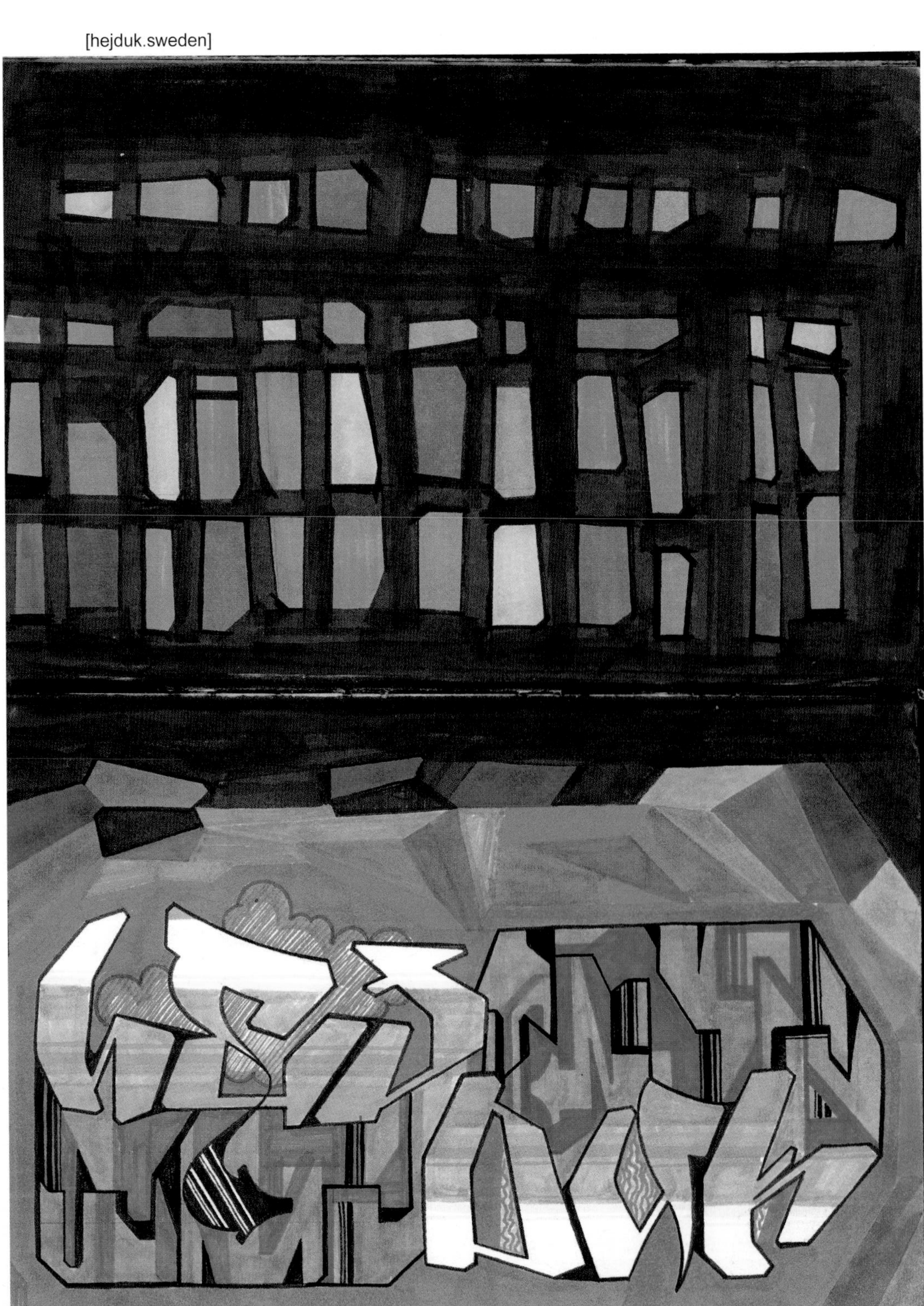

[judas.sweden]

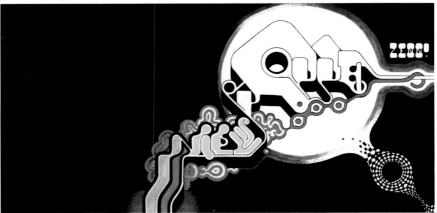

[pike.sweden]

[gladius.sweden]

[ringo.sweden]

[porno.spain]

[dems.spain]

[zedz.amsterdam]

[syer.france]

[syer.france]

FDS.OMW

[kaos.stockholm]

[uzi.stockholm]

[jake.amsterdam]

[bates.copenhagen]

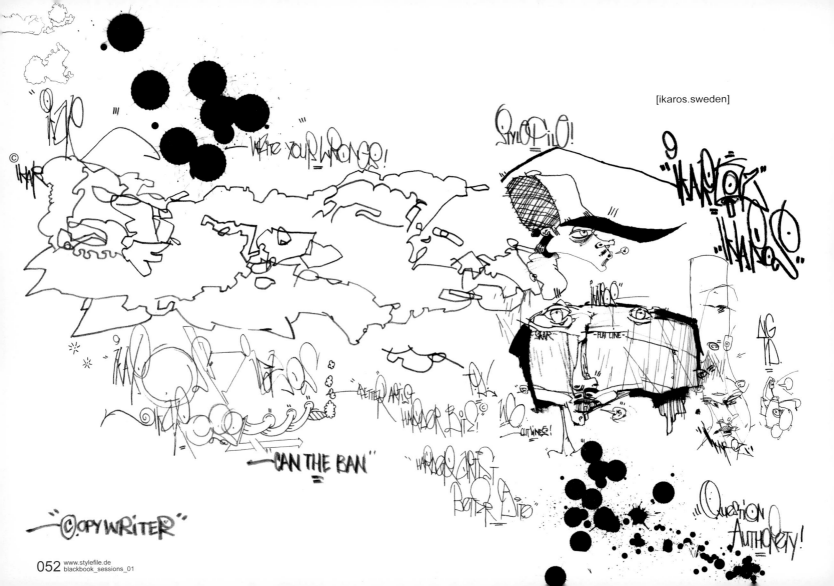

[ikaros.sweden]

SHELL BEACH

10 KELLNER für 20 LEERE TISCHE MIT GELBEN STÜHLEN

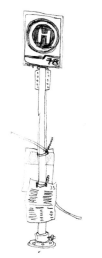

IF YOU GOT THE RIGHT ATTITUDE, INTRESTING PROBLEMS WILL FIND YOU.

DISGUSTING

TOUT VA BIEN

[hapz.hamburg]

[seemsoe.pott]

[kren]

[rough-jce_theothers.italy]

MUST Be..

[kide.berlin]

[well.berlin]

[oasis.heidelberg]

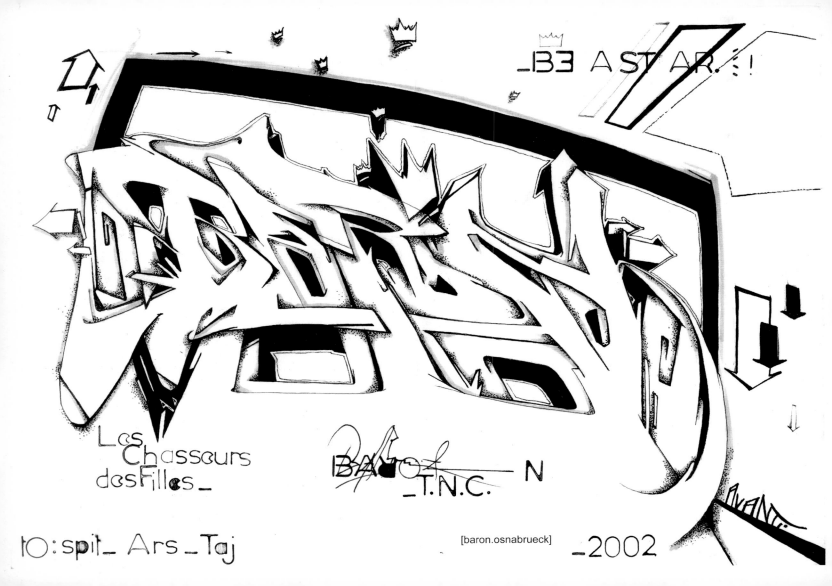

_B3 ASTAR.:!

Les Chasseurs desFilles_

BARON
_T.N.C.   N

Avant

IO:spit_ Ars_Taj

[baron.osnabrueck]   _2002

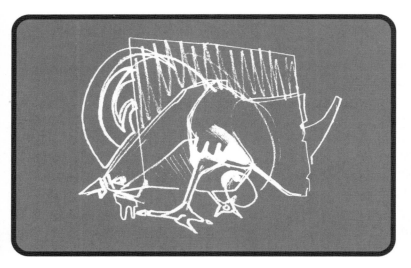

[sat.munich]

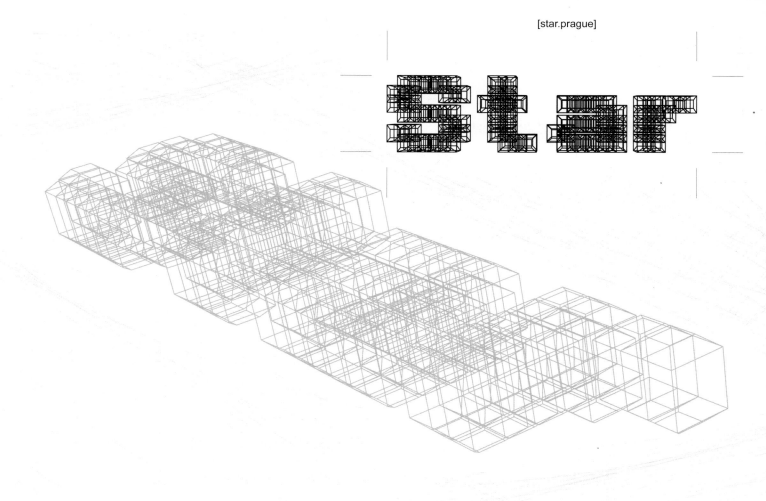

star/int/pgint@email.cz

[tour.berlin]

"one of the most BRUTAL vicious Destructive"
BOMBERS OF All TIME'S!!

CHULO. VANESSA
-7/2002!

"Sheila"

TNB.FC
BTC.TFP.

BRONX
KiLLA

KiNG'S
DESTROY!

SPEK
BTC.
RIP ★

→ GOD's OF DESTRUCTION!

[bed.bremen]

[fnack.braunschweig]

→ BY ERROR UND KARLOS.

"KIDROCK" '02

[error&karlos.osnabrueck]

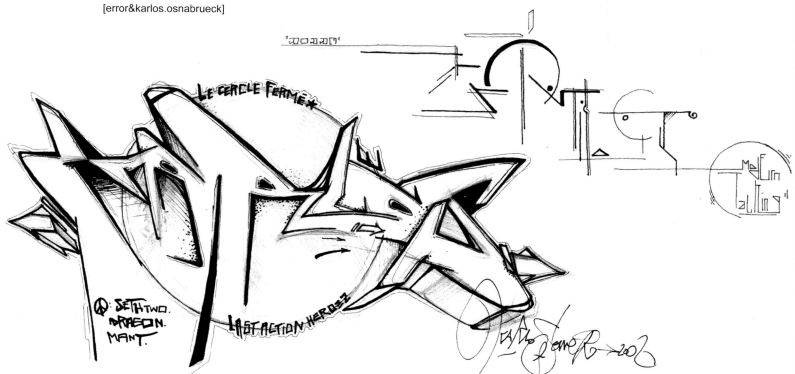

"WOADN"

LE CERCLE FERME ★

A: SETHTWO.
DRAGON.
MANT.

LAST ACTION HERO32

[stereo.gifhorn]

[ace.smash.basel]

[stuka.braunschweig]

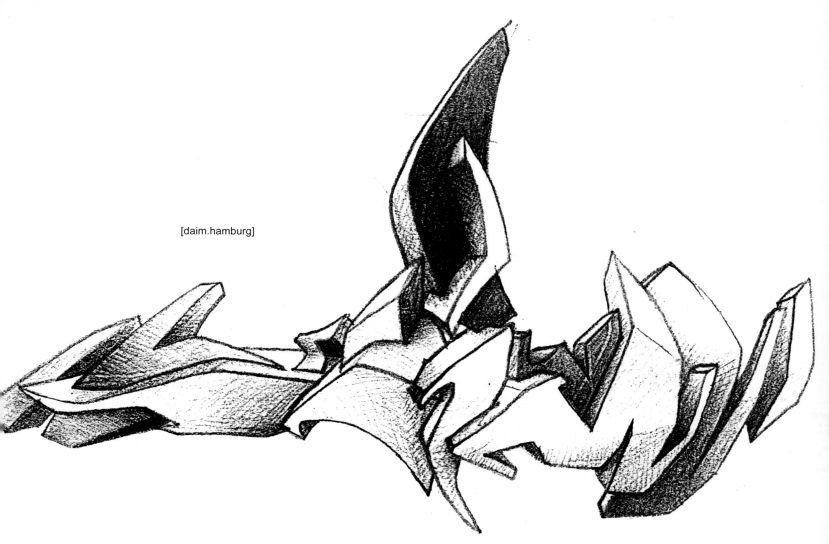

[daim.hamburg]

[dome.karlsruhe]

[ruedi.heidelberg]

[can2.mainz]

pour le maitre
mirko machines

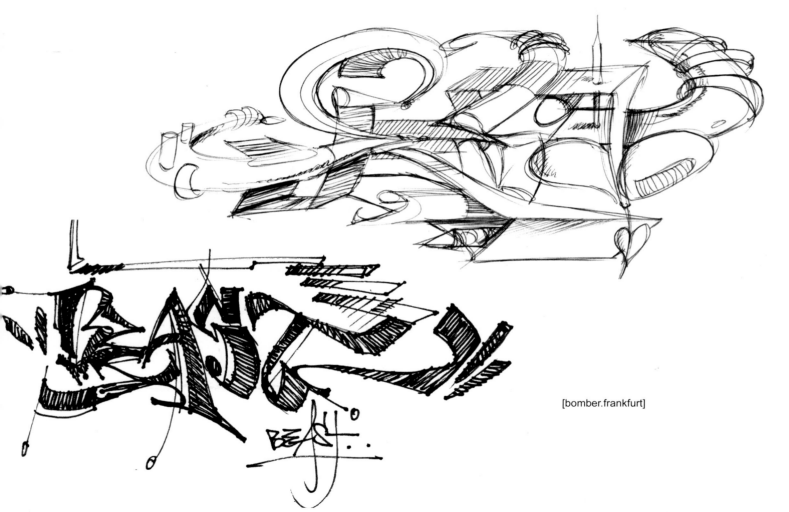

[bomber.frankfurt]

[wild&bela.offenbach]

OFFENBACH JUNE 02...

AFC RATS!!

AFC

RATS!!

[boe&sign.wiesbaden]

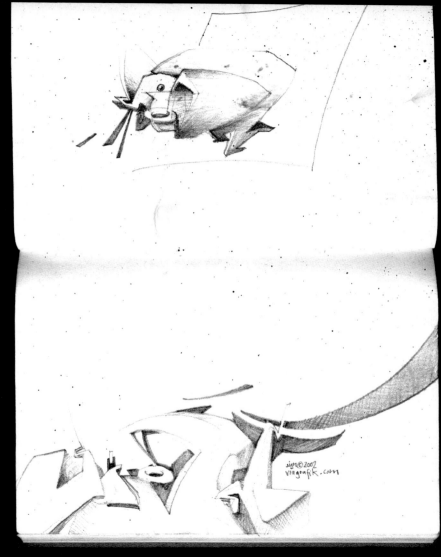

sign © 2002
viagrafik.com

[krixl.aschaffenburg]

TOGETHER! 05.2

[joan.aschaffenburg]

[blok&shok.aschaffenburg,back in the 90's]

[mohn.aschaffenburg,back in the 90's]

[bla.stuttgart]

[town.nuernberg]

[siam.munich]

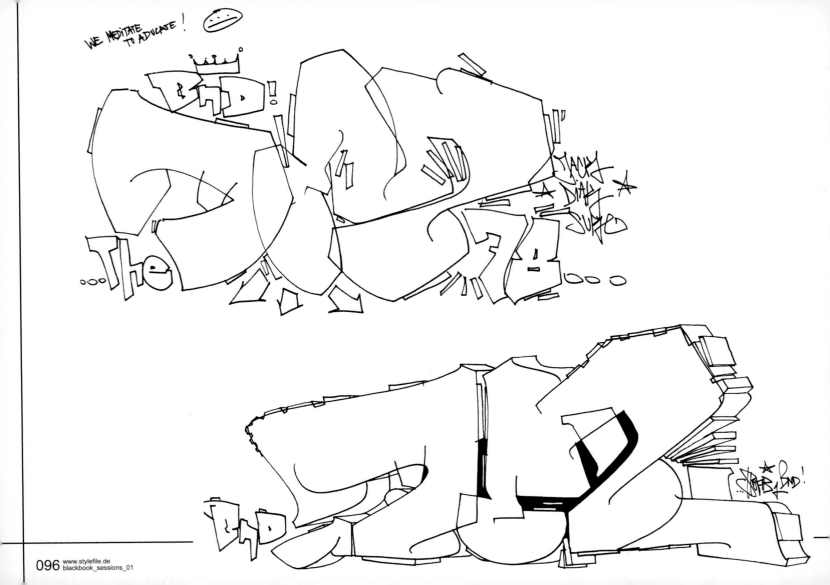

WE MEDITATE TO ADUCATE!

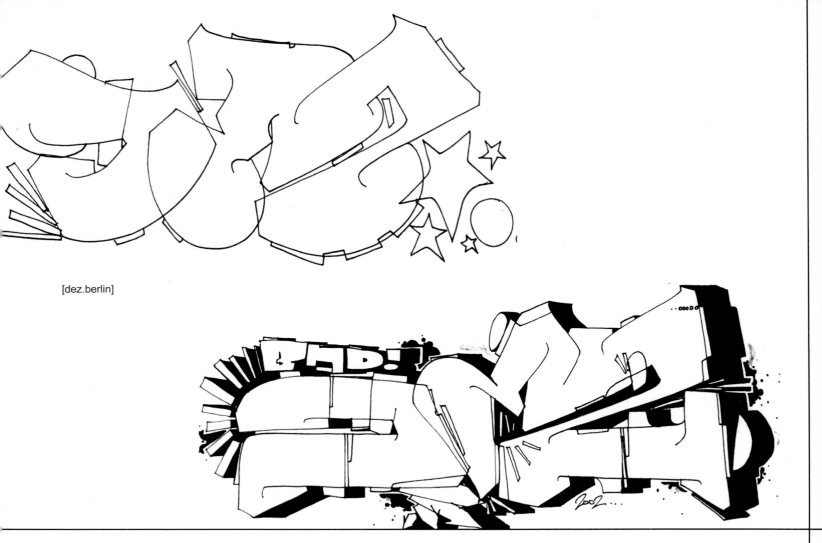

[dez.berlin]

[roche.berlin]

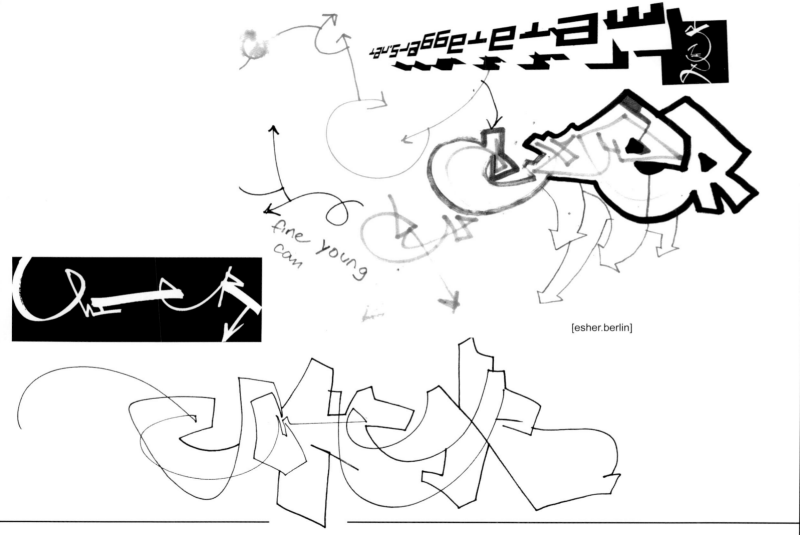

metatagger.net

fine young
con

[esher.berlin]

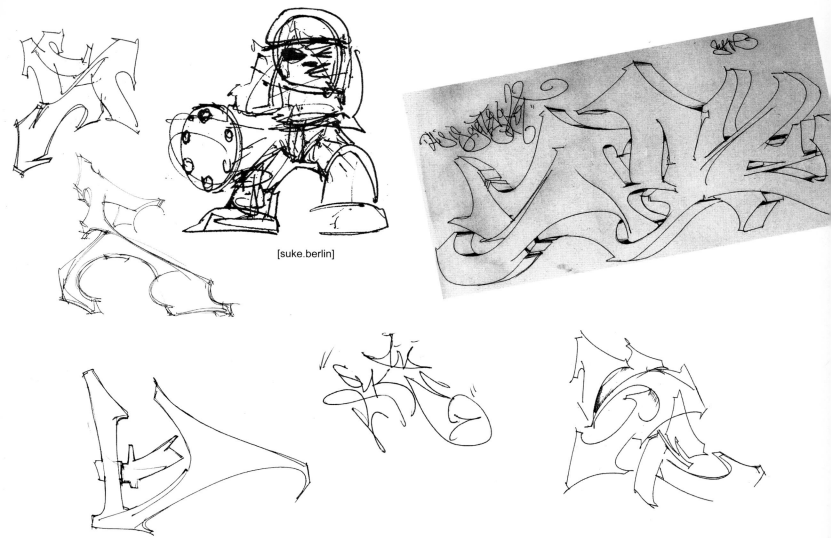

[suke.berlin]

[swet.denmark]

[zedz.amsterdam]

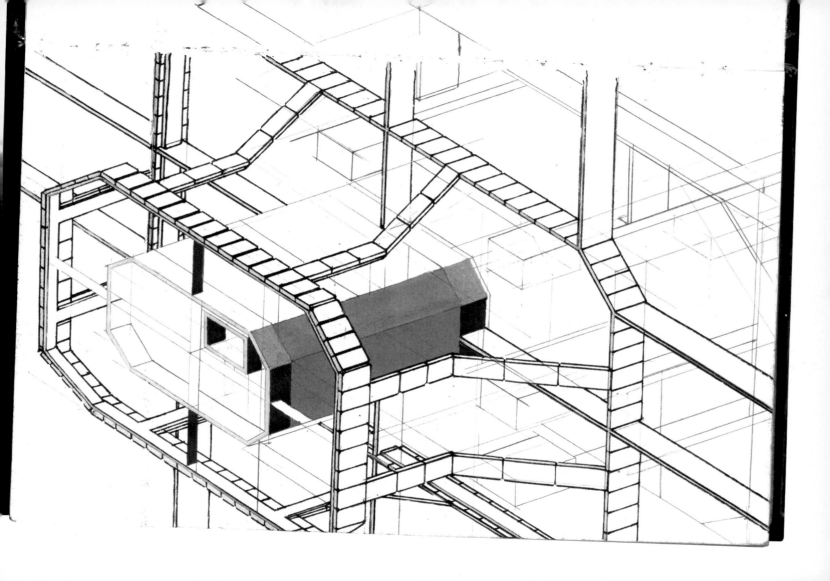

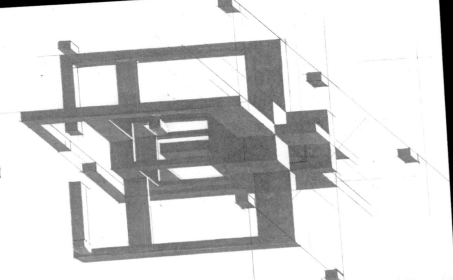

[zedz.amsterdam]

An seinem Stil herum zufeilen, wie an einem Werkstück, ist die Sehnsucht derer, die es ernst meinen. Jedoch existiert kein allgemein gültiges Rezept für einen Burner. Es gibt Dinge im Writing, die sind unmöglich zu beschreiben, weil man dem Leser nicht grenzenlose Tiefe in Wörtern erklären kann.

Trotzdem sollte es das Ziel sein, Bestimmtes zu nennen, was doch nicht gegenwärtig, sondern erst zu suchen ist.

Die menschliche Seele hat die Tendenz, nach Geschlossenheit, Ordnung und Sinn zu suchen. Unser Wissen bildet ein großes System und nur in diesem System hat das Einzelne den Wert, den wir ihm beilegen. Es lehrt uns Zusammenhänge zu verstehen und wie man „den Shit richtig kickt". Denn ein gekonnter Buchstabenstil entwickelt sich nicht in einem Vakuum, sondern setzt immer bereits ein Vorwissen voraus. Seit etwa 35 Jahren ist von Writern eine Vielfalt an Elementen, in Verbindung mit den Buchstaben entwickelt worden, die so vorher in der Normschrift nicht zu finden waren. Erst durch stilistische Experimente stoßen wir vom Bekannten zum bisher Unbekannten vor. Ausgehend von dem Grundgedanken, seinen Namen zu schreiben, werden Prozesse des Forschens ausgelöst und Strukturen der Gestaltung und Ästhetik aufgelöst. Diese gehen in neue Strukturen der Gestaltung über. (An dieser Stelle möchte ich auf eine aktuelle Entwicklung in einigen Städten Europas, dem Trend den Namen durch ein Symbol zu ersetzen, verweisen.) Doch ist die stilistische Vielfalt im sogenannten Graffiti, weltweit auf ein Bündel von Oberbegriffen zuzuordnen (Simpelstyle, Wildstyle, 3-D Style, Blockbuster etc..) die es erlauben, ein Muster erkennen zu lassen, zu welcher Stilkategorie der jeweilige Schriftzug gehört. Es ist durchaus nicht selbstverständlich, Vielfalt auf eine relative Einheit zurückzuführen, die den Umkreis von sogenannten Schmiereien absteckt. Diese Oberbegriffe sind nur die „direkte" Art, etwas zu bezeichnen, denn was wir noch am besten können, ist beurteilen oder urteilen, besser sogar als verstehen, was es z.B. mit einem Wildstyle auf sich hat. Worum geht es bei dieser Bezeichnung? Kann ein einfacher Stil auch ein wilder sein?

Einen Stil zu lesen, sollte als Aufgabe empfunden werden, die zu lösen ist. Etwas, das überwunden werden sollte, um die objektive Urteilskraft zu stärken. Diese Aufgabe verlangt vom Betrachter eine Entscheidung. Jeder Stil, sei er klar oder abstrakt, verursacht je nach seiner Gestaltung eine mehr oder weniger innere Spannung beim Betrachter. So wird die Aufgabe von einem als leicht und angenehm lesbar empfunden, während jemand anderes diesen Stil für außerordentlich schwer zu entziffern hält. Was sagt uns das?

Bei dem ersten Kontakt mit einem „Graffiti-Stil" erlebt der Betrachter fast ausnahmslos das Vorhandensein oder das Fehlen von Gestaltungseigenschaften. Der Schriftzug z.B. wird als „sinnlos, ungegliedert, unbegrenzt, offen u.s.w." erlebt und gleichzeitig als schwer auffaßbar. Dies drückt eine Art Klage darüber aus, dass die für den Betrachter unbedingt notwendigen positiven Gestaltungsmomente fehlen. Natürlich offenbaren sie sich manchmal nicht beim ersten Blick. Man muß sich der Sache stellen und versuchen herauszufinden, wo derjenige seine Schwerpunkte bei der Gestaltung seines Schriftzuges gesetzt hat. Dann erst erkennt man die wahren Qualitäten eines Schriftzuges, ob derjenige nur auf tolle Effekte wert gelegt hat oder ob er probiert eine alles beinhaltende Komplexität zu erreichen. Tiefe ist grenzenlos. Da ein Writer eine Seele hat, kann sie sich also auch in seinem Stil wieder finden. Die Möglichkeiten sind grenzenlos. Ein Buchstabenstil sollte eine gewisse Charakteristik vorweisen, um seiner Existenzberechtigung willen, in der Kunst.

Generell neigt der Mensch dazu, erst den ganzen Schriftzug mit dem Auge zu umfahren und das Ganze in einer unmittelbar erlebten Ganzqualität zu erfassen. Geschlossenheit und Komplexität eines Stils wirken bestimmend auf den Betrachter. Je stärker diese Komponenten vorhanden sind, umso feiner wird er betrachtet! Denn der Mensch hat meist den Drang, dem Sinnlosen einen Sinn zuzuordnen. Ein mittelmäßig gekonnter Stil eines Writers z.B. zeichnet sich dadurch aus, dass zwei oder drei spezifische Stellen in seinem Schriftzug hervorgehoben werden und als angenehm empfunden werden, während die übrigen im Schriftzug unbeachtet bleiben (aus welchem Grund auch immer), ohne den Gesamteindruck zu bestimmen. Es bleibt sozusagen ein Rest, der in das Ganze nicht einbezogen wird, was die Funktionalität betrifft. Dadurch entsteht eine Instabilität, hervorgerufen durch eine Isolation von einzelnen Stücken im Schriftzug. Man muss verstehen, dass beim Buchstabendesign Sinn und Gestalt innigst gebunden sind. Sinnvolle Buchstabenstile werden meist sicherer und genauer aufgefasst und verglichen als sinnarme. Dieser vom Ganzen bestimmte Sinn drängt sich auf und verleiht Sicherheit. Die Ausnahme bestätigt natürlich auch hier die Regel. Abschließend möchte ich noch erwähnen, dass nicht umsonst viele Writer der Auffassung sind, dass es die hohe Kunst des Buchstabendesigns ist, einen guten Simplestyle zu malen, der ohne viel Schnick-Schnack auskommt und trotzdem alles verbrennt, was ihm sozusagen übergeordnet ist.
Peace I'm out.

MY BOOK OF STYLE

To cut on a style, like on a workpiece, is the yearning of the ones who take it seriously. But there is no recipe for a burner. There are things in writing that can not be described, because you can´t explain endless deepness to a reader in words. But still it should be the goal to call it a definete, what is not yet existing, but still something to look for. The human soul has the tendence to seek for unity, order and sense. Our knowledge forms a system and only in this system single things get the value we want it to have. It teaches us to understand connections and how to kick the shit right. To evole a masterly letterstyle does not come out of a vacuum, but needs knowledge even before. Since 35 years, there is large variety of elements, connected to letters, that were not existing in normal writing before. Only by stilistic experiments we get from the unknown to the new. Beginning from the thought of writing your name, processes of research are being started and structures of shaping and aesthetics evolve into new structures of shaping. (here i´d like to refer to evolvement in some major cities, the trend to put a symbol for your name.) but stylistic varieties in so-called graffiti is bound to collection of generic terms (simplestyle, wildstyle, 3-d, blockbuster…) which allows to see a pattern of which the style belongs to. But it is not always easy to bring variety back to a relative unity, which takes it away

from so-called scribblings. Those generic terms are only the direct art of describing something. What we can do best is to judge, even better than to understand what is meant by a wildstyle. What is this term about? Can a simplestyle be wild, too? To even read a style should be considered as a task, that is to be mastered. Something that should be done to strenghten your objective judgement. This task needs a decision from the watcher. Every style, is it clear or abstract, leads to tension inside the watcher. So, the task is judged as something easy and nice readable while someone else tells you that this style is extraordinary hard to read. What does this show to us? At first contact with a graffiti style, the viewer sees missing or not missing elements. The style is judged as sense-less, open and unlimited and so on, and at the same time hard to connect to. This reveals that the viewer misses important elements of shape. Of course you

don't always miss them at the first time, you have to take the challenge and try to find out where this someone has concentrated on with his shapes. Then you can realize where qualities of the style are set. Did he concentrate on nice effects or did he try to reach for complexitivity? Deepness is endless, while a writer has a soul, you can find it in his style.
Possibilities are not restricted. A letterstyle should put on a characteristic to set its right to exist in art. Generally man tends to surround the style with his eyes and to see the whole thing in a direct experienced quality. Unity and complexitivity of a style are most attracting to a viewer. The stronger these elements exist, the more closely it is viewed. Man has the urge to give a sense to the senseless. A mediocre ability of shaping a style shows that a writer has put his accents to 2 or 3 different places in his style and that those are being accepted as neat, while the other

ones stay unrealized (no matter why), without determing the whole expression. What stays at rest is what remains unconnected in regards of function. An insta-bility caused by an isolation of single parts in the piece. You have to understand that sense and shape is deeply connected in design of letters. Letterstyles with sense are mostly viewed more closely and more secure than senseless ones. The sense determined by the whole leads to security. The exception determines the rule. Finally I want to say that many writers have the opinion that it is the high art of designing a letter to create a good simplestyle which can exist without any poppycock and still burns everything that is put above. Peace I am out

the prototype issue
started_by_suke_chill_flash

**the second attack by
tape_metro**

blue_solostrike by
==> ruzd

todays firestarter
bird_agit_minimax

... Like the Snowtime.....

WE LOVE IT...

"LIMITS" KAOS

their definition of snow
gum_kaos_dream

**natures comback supported by
smash_joan_silk**

joan_02
springfile

the unstoppable sand.soldiers
face_jeru_odin

VISUAL.POWERMOVES

performed by

WISE
CAGE
KACAO77
SHAW
KIDE
DES
2COLD80
JACK
OTIS
SUCK
GINA
CHAZ
DIAK

2001
L. iN. M.

PHAT SHOUT OUT'Z TO KBRSIO77, PHOBY, D-KYE, SHOW, DHOR, ZEAL, ... BOES II ... HEK 36, girls, girls, girls ... SEE YA NEXT YEAR,

"2COLD 80TH "2001"

2001...

"RETURN TO ZERO"

"2 COLD 80TH"

2001 ...

yo:VALE.Twix.Jnce.Jak.MosfA
FisK.PtiF. SAFPR

life|visual|style

..prepare yourself for one of your most exciting moments in life!
WWW.MONTANA-CANS.COM

L&G Vertriebs GmbH
Postfach 10 25 47
69015 Heidelberg
Tel: +49/ 6221/ 36 333 30
Fax +49/ 6221/ 36 333 33
sales@montana-cans.com

sketch made by KACAO 77 member of
the MONTANA Writer Team

[lord_scan.aachen]

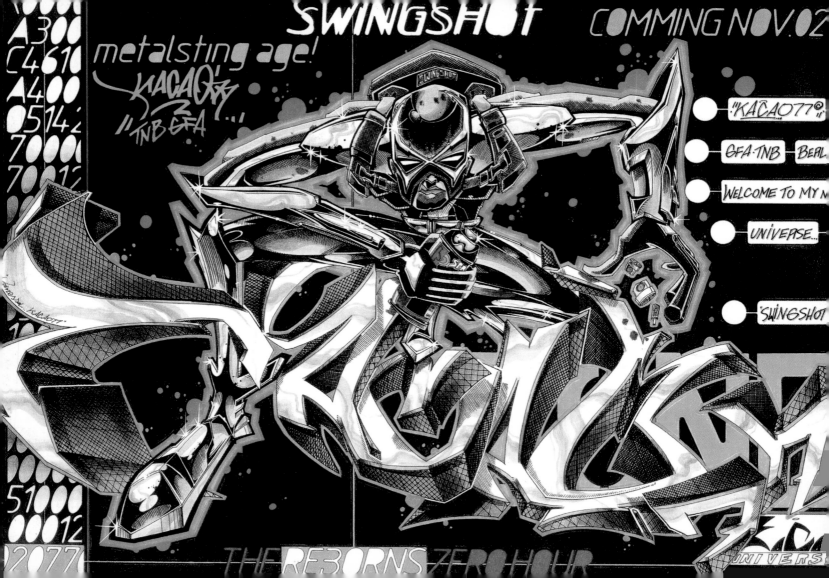

[fury.new_zealand]

DREAM YOUR DREAMS...

LIVE YOUR DREAMS

AND YOUR LIFE WILL BE YOUR DREAM

..KEEPIN' THE SPIRIT ALIVE !

Jetzt Gratiskatalog anfordern unter Tel.: 0231 - 93 71 11-12
Order your free catalog: +49 231 - 93 71 11-12
www.stickupkidz.com

prototypefile / 11.1999

secondfile / 03.2000

bluefile / 07.2000

firefile / 11.2000

greyfile / 03.2001

winefile / 07.2001

snowfile / 11.2001

springfile / 03.2002

desertfile / 07.2002

silverfile / 11.2002

ISBN: 3-980-7478-0-8

surf the city / 11.2000

ISBN: 3-980-7478-1-6

END2ENDS

on the wheels of steel... e2es / 03.2002

GRAFFITICALENDAR 2002

graffiti-calendars

<2002

2003>

GRAFFITICALENDAR 2003

stylefile
BLACKBOOK.SESSIONS
>>editorial<<

distribution
joern@stylefile.de
editor & layout
krixl@stylefile.de
support
seb - zicki - gotcha - arnd
translation
mikeymeik

Of course we have to thank all of the writers printed in this book! Beside of that, we have to give props to a handfull of very special-supporters! Without their work, this book would not have been possible....

KAKAO77 and the whole visual.team for their study of style
SHAW.SHORTCUT for terrorising berlin
SUKE & JACK für die geilen ess-unterlagen
the incredible JYMBONIZER for his extra-extra-long-sketch
king KAOS45 for his wise words and fresh styles
ESHER for the first scribbles we got
ZEDZ for leaving his books to me
TOBIAS from Stockholm for his support
DAIM for his contacts
AIR33 (www.air33.org) of Trendsetterz (http://trendsetterz.weblogger.com) for correcting our english
this guy called DARE for all he did for us...
THANXXX!

Copyright (c) 2002
No part of this book may be
reproduced in any manner
without written permission by
PUBLIKAT KG and/ or the artists.

>>>>>> **For details and further publications check www.stylefile.de!**

for information get in touch with **PUBLIKAT KG**,
fon: +49 (0) 60 21 / 90 04 0-0, fax: +49 (0) 60 21 / 90 04 0-20,
contact@eightmileshigh.de, www.eightmileshigh.de
switzerland: +41 (0) 61 / 64 39 420, info@nr-1.ch
spain: +34 (0) 91 / 55 70 230, orbital@arrakis.es

EIGHT|MILES|HIGH
urbanstreetwear
made 2 survive in this grey world